The Ocean World

BY PETER RYAN

COLOUR ILLUSTRATIONS BY

LUDEK PESEK

A PUFFIN ORIGINAL

PENGUIN BOOKS

Explorer 5

ACKNOWLEDGEMENTS

The publishers and the author would like to thank the following for their kind permission to reproduce the photographs appearing in this book:

Jon Brenneis, p. 36; Michel Brigaud, Electricité de France, p. 5; Institute of Geological Sciences, pp. 22 and 23; N.A.S.A., pp. 3 and 45; Les Requins Associés, Groupe Cousteau, p. 13; Siebe-Gorman Ltd, p. 9; Teledine Explorations Co., p. 21; U.S.I.S., p. 17.

For Lucy Cussans and Lucy Goodman

Puffin Books: a Division of Penguin Books Ltd, Harmondsworth, Middlesex
Penguin Books Inc, 7110 Ambassador Road, Baltimore, Maryland 21207, USA.
Penguin Books Australia Ltd, Ringwood, Victoria, Australia

First published 1973

Copyright © Peter Ryan, 1973
Colour illustrations © Ludek Pesek, 1973

Black and white diagrams ©Penguin Education, 1973

Made and printed in Holland by Drukkerij de Lange van Leer N.V.,
Amsterdam and Deventer
Set in Monophoto Plantin

Apollo Splashdown

An Underwater World

Splashdown in the Pacific at the end of a 384,000 kilometre (240,000 mile) journey to the moon. Yet only 6 kilometres (3.75 miles) beneath the Apollo spaceship lies an underwater world every bit as fascinating and unexplored as the surface of the moon. The Pacific Ocean is just one of the oceans and seas which cover more than 70 per cent of the surface area of our planet.

Many centuries have passed since man first put to sea, yet today only a few men and women have ventured down into the 1,352,000,000 cubic kilometres (330,000,000 cubic miles) of salt water that encloses this hidden world beneath the waves.

3

Our distant ancestors first saw the sea when they began to explore the coastline of their first home, Africa. For them it was a place of refuge from hungry wild animals, but it was also a barrier of water, to be crossed by raft or dugout canoe in search of new lands. Today the oceans are much more to man than a highway between continents; they have become an important source of food, energy and minerals.

We catch more than 240 million tonnes of fish each year, but that is only a tiny fraction of the food we need to feed a hungry world. When we come to understand more about the home and habits of fish, how they move around the oceans and what influences them to gather in certain areas, the fishing nets will be fuller, and one day we may even be able to farm fish just as we have learned to raise cattle and grow crops instead of hunting for our food.

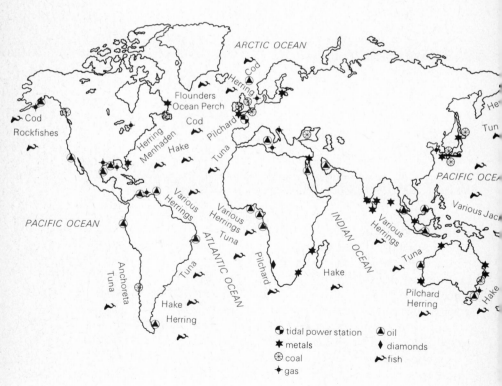

ARCTIC OCEAN

Cod
Herring

Flounders
Ocean Perch

Cod
Rockfishes

Cod

Pilchard

Herring
Menhaden

Hake

Tuna

Tun

Various
Herrings

Various
Herrings

Cod

Tuna

PACIFIC OCEAN

Various Jac

PACIFIC OCEAN

INDIAN OCEAN

Various
Herrings

ATLANTIC OCEAN

Tuna

Pilchard

Hake

Tuna

Anchoreta
Tuna

Tuna

Hake

Pilchard
Herring

Hake

Hake

Herring

🌀 tidal power station   🔵 oil

✹ metals   ◆ diamonds

⊕ coal   ➳ fish

✦ gas

4

We can also make use of the natural energy of the oceans as a source of power. In France a power station has recently been built which uses the rise and fall of the tide to generate electricity. It is the first plant of its kind and, as it uses no fuel, promises a future of cheap power for coastal areas.

From beneath the sea bed we are extracting oil and gas. Other valuable mineral deposits, including mud-and-sand sediments rich in diamonds, gold, silver and tin, copper, lead, zinc and iron, lie undiscovered on or below the ocean floor. The map opposite shows what we use today from the oceans, but this is only a beginning. As long as the population of our planet continues to increase, so does our need to explore and develop the oceans and their riches.

A photograph of the French tidal power station between St Malo and Dinard in Brittany. The open sea is at the top of the picture.

A Viking ship crossing the North Atlantic to Greenland ▶

The Pioneers

The Vikings who sailed across the uncharted North Atlantic from Scandinavia were among the first people to realize that the surface of the earth is mostly water. Until the Vikings set sail, the map-makers of Europe had pictured a world of mainly dry land stretching from Ireland to China.

In those days many people believed the world was flat, and captains of ships planning voyages of discovery had to convince their crews that they would not fall off the edge. Then, in 1522, ships of the Portuguese explorer Magellan finished a three-year voyage round the world. He sailed off the left-hand edge of the maps of the day and reappeared at the right-hand edge, near the Philippines, thereby convincing most people that the earth is a sphere. The maps were redrawn, and have been redrawn many times since then. The maps we have today show the knowledge accumulated from many such voyages across unknown oceans and along remote and dangerous coastlines.

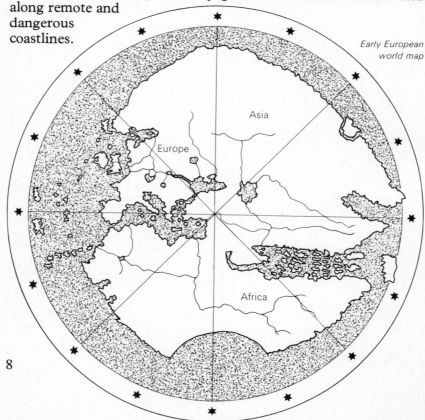

Early European world map

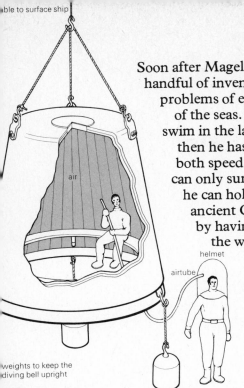

air

helmet

airtube

weights to keep the
diving bell upright

Diving bell

Soon after Magellan's ships were safely home, a handful of inventors turned their talents to the problems of exploration beneath the surface of the seas. Early man certainly learned to swim in the lakes and rivers of Africa. Since then he has perfected his style in terms of both speed and distance, but, unaided, he can only survive under water for as long as he can hold his breath. The adventurous ancient Greeks got round this difficulty by having themselves lowered beneath the waves in barrels full of air, but it proved risky, and the air was soon used up. It was not until the sixteenth century, and the invention of the diving bell, that men were able to spend more than an hour under water.

*Modern diving suit being tested
in a tank full of water*

The next important development in underwater exploration was the air-tight diving suit, invented by a German, Augustus Siebe, in 1837. It enabled men to venture beyond the safety of the diving bell with a supply of air pumped down to the diver from a ship afloat on the surface.

Then, in the early 1940s, a Frenchman, Jacques-Yves Cousteau, produced the aqualung, which freed the diver from the need of an air supply pumped down from above. The aqualung provides him with an air supply, compressed into bottles, that he can carry strapped on to his back.

Modern aqualung divers around Jacques Cousteau's Conshelf ▶

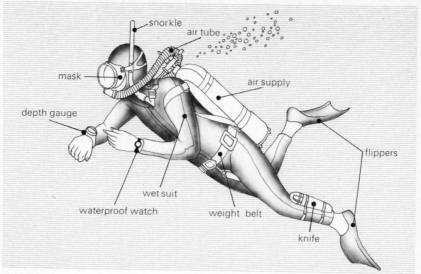

Aqualung

The availability of the aqualung, and its relative cheapness, has greatly increased the number of professional underwater explorers, and during the last few years great strides forward have been made.

Jacques-Yves Cousteau is probably one of the greatest pioneers of underwater exploration, and is constantly trying to find ways by which man can become a permanent inhabitant of the under-water world.

In 1963 he built an experimental three-house underwater 'village', called Conshelf 2, on the floor of the Red Sea off the Sudan. Two of the houses were placed at a depth of 10 metres (33 feet), while the third shelter was lowered to 26 metres (85 feet) below the surface. Headquarters of Conshelf 2 was one of the two shallow buildings, called Starfish House, which is shown on pages 10 and 11. Every day the inhabitants put on their aqualungs and spent several hours exploring the surroundings of their underwater house. The experiment was a success, and proved that men and women could live and work underwater for weeks at a time.

With an aqualung, an experienced diver can easily reach a depth of about 50 metres (about 160 feet), but below this level pressure makes breathing difficult. At these depths, oxygen becomes 'stronger', and tends to make the diver feel lightheaded. The other main component of the air we breathe, nitrogen, begins to be dissolved by the blood, and when the diver returns to the surface there is a danger that the dissolved nitrogen may boil out of his blood in the same way that carbon dioxide comes bubbling out of a bottle of fizzy drink. This causes great pain, and can result in permanent injury to the diver. So, for deep dives with an aqualung, a different air mixture is used. The mixture contains less oxygen than normal air, and the nitrogen is replaced by helium, which is not dissolved by the blood. In 1956, a British naval officer, George Wookey, using an oxygen-helium mixture, reached a depth of 170 metres (600 feet) in Oslo Fjord, Norway.

In 1972 the French carried out an experiment to find out how deep man can safely dive using this mixture. They built a sealed chamber, on dry land, in which volunteers spent several days. The pressure was slowly built up to that found more than 600 metres (2,000 feet) down in the sea, the volunteers breathing the oxygen-helium mixture. The experiment was a great success, and one day soon divers, equipped with special aqualungs, called electrolungs, which gradually adjust the breathing mixture as they descend, will be able to work without too much danger at these new depths.

Manned descents below these levels are possible in a number of small submarines. Cousteau's diving saucer, for example, garaged in the second shallow house of the Conshelf village, can take two men down to 300 metres (about 1,000 feet). The saucer cabin is sealed and kept at normal atmospheric pressure to prevent breathing problems.

Cousteau's saucer

Trieste descending the Challenger Deep ▶

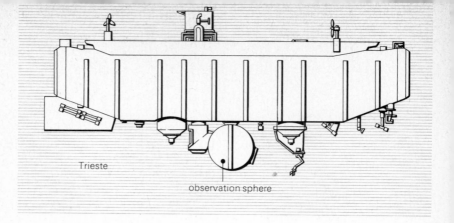

Trieste

observation sphere

To explore the deepest ocean valleys, or trenches as they are called, we need diving vessels with very thick hulls. In 1960, a Swiss, Jacques Piccard, and an American, Donald Walsh, in *Trieste* (above), reached a depth of 11,000 metres (in fact, 35,800 feet) in the Challenger Deep, part of the Marianas Trench in the Pacific Ocean off Guam. This is only seventy metres or so above the world's deepest ocean floor, which has been discovered, since 1960, in the same trench. The main trenches of the world's oceans are shown on the map on page 20. Regular trips to these depths will probably be possible in the future, but today there are many small manned research submarines which can reach the rest of the ocean floor. Some of these are shown below.

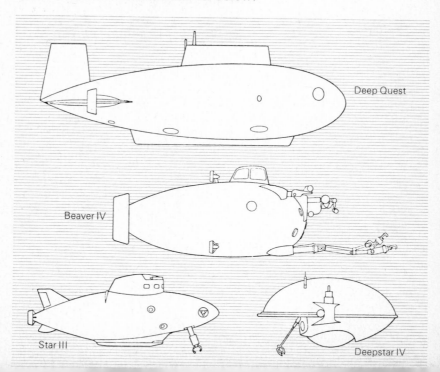

Deep Quest

Beaver IV

Star III

Deepstar IV

In 1966, *Aluminaut* (below, photographed under water) was used to recover a hydrogen bomb which sank in 765 metres (2,500 feet) of water off the Mediterranean coast of Spain when an American Air Force bomber crashed. The operation cost $30,000,000 (about £12,500,000).

Aluminaut

Underwater exploration, like space travel, is very expensive, and though man can descend to almost any part of the ocean he chooses, machines can often do the job much more cheaply and efficiently. Television cameras can replace man for much exploratory work, such as locating wrecks for salvage, or making detailed studies of the sea bed.

As well as cameras, man can employ all sorts of machines to help him explore beneath the waves. There are echo sounders, temperature readers, current meters, bottom dredgers, and sediment corers, feeding back information that would take hours of hazardous work by deep-sea divers.

17

An imaginary view of the Atlantic Ocean basin drained of water ▶

The Sea Floor

continental shelf
main trenches

Continental shelves and trenches

The sea floor is not just a great basin between land masses: it is a rugged valley full of hills and mountains. To get a better idea of what the sea floor looks like, let us pretend that we can drain away the water from the Atlantic Ocean. The colour picture on pages 18-19 shows an imaginary view of the Canary Islands, off the north-west coast of Africa, rising as high volcanic mountains from the floor of the dried-up Atlantic. In the right foreground you can see part of the continental shelf of Africa, and if you look at the map above you will see that there is a continental shelf forming an underwater extension of all the continents. This shelf varies in width from 0–1,500 kilometres (937 miles), occupying an area equal to 18 per cent of all the dry land of the earth. The Atlantic part of the shelf is shown in the photograph of the relief map on pages 22–23. The shelf varies in depth from 20 metres (65 feet) to 550 metres (1,798 feet), which is easily within the range of manned submarine exploration.

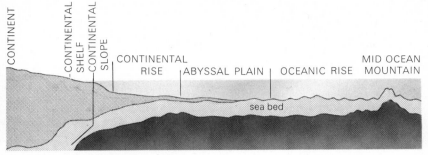

Section across a typical ocean floor

As you can see in the diagram above, the continental shelf ends in a steep slope, which lies about 4 kilometres (2.5 miles) below the surface of the ocean. From here on the slope called the continental rise is more gentle, leading to the abyssal plain, around 6 kilometres (3.75 miles) down, and occupying more than 40 per cent of the ocean floor. As we cross this plain, the sea floor begins to rise again where we meet the oceanic rise, which leads up to a long ridge of underwater mountains. On the relief map of the Atlantic you can see these mountains stretching from Iceland to the South Atlantic. The photograph below shows part of the mid-Atlantic mountain system. The picture was made by bouncing sound waves off the sea floor and recording them aboard a surface ship.

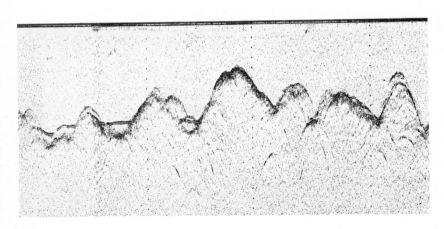

Mid-Atlantic mountain

21

Relief map of the Atlantic Ocean floor ▶

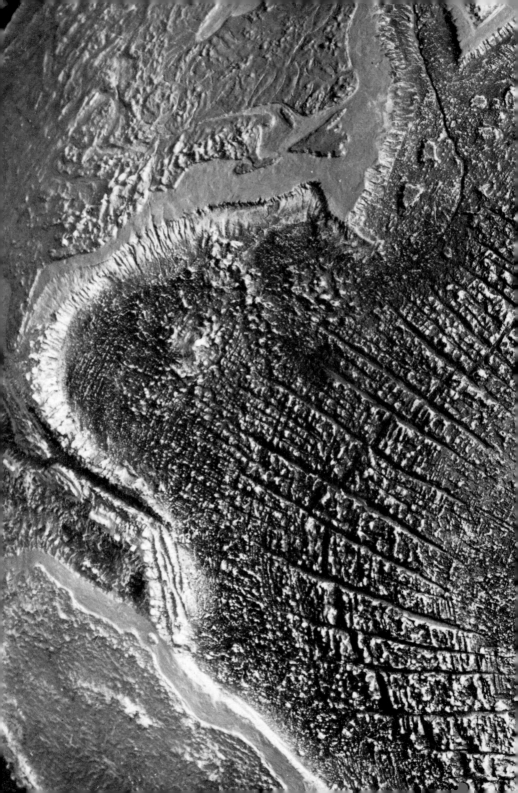

These mid-ocean mountain ridges are very interesting because they are the birthplace of new ocean floor. In 1912 a German scientist, Alfred Wegener, upset many of the other great scientists of his day by suggesting that the continents were slowly drifting around and bumping into each other, like a giant mobile jigsaw puzzle. Since then, and particularly in the last few years, many scientists who have been studying these mid-ocean mountains have come to believe that he was probably right. The jigsaw puzzle is moved a few centimetres each year by very slow earth movements deep beneath the continents and ocean floors. These slow earth movements operate a system of conveyor belts, which, over millions of years, has greatly changed the map of the world. The diagram below shows how this system works. The conveyor belts operate in pairs. They begin by bringing up new sea floor from beneath the mid-ocean mountains, which pushes the older sea floor to each side. This explains why the pattern of the floor of the Atlantic Ocean shown on the relief map looks symmetrical.

At the other end of the conveyor belt the older sea floor plunges back down into the earth, and this is where we often find the deep ocean trenches like the one visited by the *Trieste*. Sometimes the conveyor belts run into each other. If they are carrying ocean floor, it disappears down into the deep trenches. If they are carrying a piece of continent, the material gets crumpled up to form mountains. The diagram opposite shows an imaginary slice through the earth where oceans are growing and trenches and mountains forming.

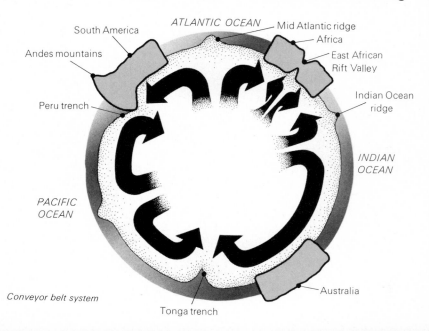

Conveyor belt system

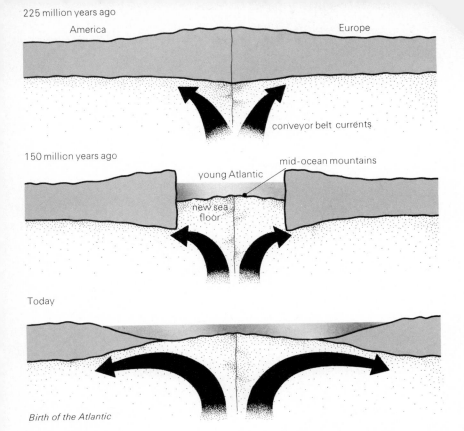

225 million years ago

America

Europe

conveyor belt currents

150 million years ago

mid-ocean mountains

young Atlantic

new sea floor

Today

Birth of the Atlantic

The diagram above shows how the conveyor belt system gave birth to the Atlantic Ocean around 225 million years ago. Since that time the Atlantic has been growing wider at the rate of a few centimetres each year. Today a new pair of conveyor belts is at work beneath Africa and may, one day in the distant future, open up the East African Rift Valley to form a new ocean.

Water

When you turn the page you will see an imaginary view of New York under 75 metres (245 feet) of water. This dramatic picture could only be seen in the unlikely event of the polar ice caps melting.

25

Artist's impression of New York under water ▶

The artist chose New York because it is built on a small island surrounded by water. Would your home survive a 75 metre rise in sea level? You might like to redraw the map of your country using the 75-metre contour line in your atlas, as the new coastline. This gives us some idea of the amount of water trapped as ice at the North and South Poles. This extra 75 metres (245 feet) of water, suddenly released into the oceans of the world, would have a catastrophic effect on the amount of dry land left for us to live on.

The polar ice, and the currents of cold water it produces in the oceans, also has a great effect on the world's weather. Every day 875 cubic kilometres (214 cubic miles) of water is evaporated from the oceans to form clouds. Of this, 775 cubic kilometres (189 cubic miles) falls back into the sea as rain. The remaining 100 cubic kilometres (25 cubic miles) is carried by winds to fall over land. It is eventually returned to the oceans by rivers. The diagram below shows how the world's water supply is constantly circulating.

The winds that carry the daily 100 cubic kilometres of rain over the land are either warmed or cooled by the temperature of the ocean water. This is why the British Isles have a warmer climate than eastern Canada, though they are both the same distance from the equator. The Gulf Stream, coming from the south, warms the waters of the Atlantic to the west of the British Isles, while the Labrador Current, coming from the north, cools the coastal waters of eastern Canada. The next diagram shows the main warm and cold currents which control the weather of coastal areas.

Water circulation

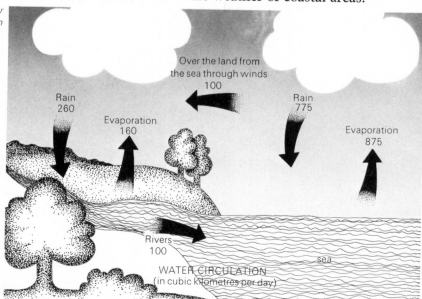

Over the land from the sea through winds 100

Rain 260

Evaporation 160

Rain 775

Evaporation 875

Rivers 100

sea

WATER CIRCULATION
(in cubic kilometres per day)

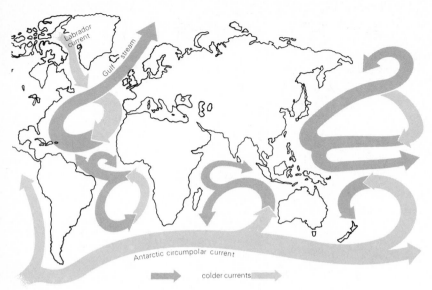

Labrador current

Gulf stream

Antarctic circumpolar current

colder currents

Warm and cold currents of the world's oceans

Warm water is lighter than cold water and tends to float above it. Warm water currents are therefore near the surface of the oceans, while cold currents run deeper. Fresh water is lighter than salty water, which tends to sink. In the sunny Mediterranean evaporation makes the water very salty, and the sea would dry up if fresher water did not flow in from the Atlantic above the current of saltier water which flows out underneath it.

Currents, warm, cold, salty and fresh, are constantly mixing and stirring the oceans, bringing warm weather from the equator and coolness from the poles. Enormous volumes of water are carried by currents. The Antarctic Circumpolar Current carries about 900 cubic metres (9,500 cubic feet) of water around the southern tip of South America every second. These currents also ensure a constant flow of nutrients from the sea bed to the ocean surface on which the plant life of the sea depends. The fish feed on these plants and so, in their turn, these currents are very important to man. A better understanding of how they work would mean more accurate weather forecasting and more productive fishing. Today both surface ships and submarines are being used to follow and chart the pathways of the ocean currents.

29

A view from a space station of the future showing the irrigation of part of the Sahara Desert ▶

If you look again at the diagram on page 28, you will see that the oceans provide nearly two fifths of the daily amount of fresh rain-water which falls on the land areas of the world. Fresh water is vital to life. In land areas where there is very little fresh water, all kinds of life are very restricted, yet many such places are surrounded by sea. Desalination (extracting freshwater from sea water) is an expensive process, but it is getting cheaper as techniques improve, and today there are about 1,000 such plants in operation. The colour picture on pages 30 and 31 shows a plan for the future. If you look at a map of Africa, you will notice several large areas in the northern part of that continent lying below sea level. The Quattara Depression, for example, is a valley the size of Wales. Our picture shows a view from a space station looking down at such a depression near the sea sometime in the future.

Canals have been cut through the coastal mountains to channel sea water inland where nuclear-powered desalination plants are turning it into fresh water to irrigate land which was once desert.

Waves and Tides

While the ocean depths are stirred by currents, the surface waters are also on the move. Waves are caused by wind, and though the waves themselves travel great distances across the ocean, the water does not move very much. The series of three diagrams opposite shows how this happens. If you watch a gull floating in the sea on a calm day, you can see it ride the circular up and down movement of the water as a wave passes. When the sea is stormy, however, the wave movement is much greater, and waves as high as 31 metres (102 feet) have been reported.

Even larger waves are caused by underwater earthquake movements of the sea bed; these are called *tsunamis*, a Japanese word. These giant waves cross the ocean at speeds of up to 700 kilometres (437 miles) an hour, and can be nearly 67 metres (220 feet) high when they reach the shallow water off the coast. They can be very destructive. It is difficult to imagine what a 70-metre-high wave looks like, but the following colour picture will give you some idea of what a *tsunami* is, and the damage it can do.

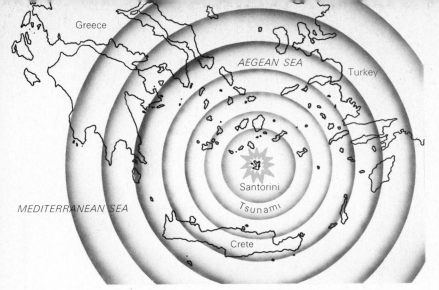

Tsunamis follow the volcanic eruption on the island of Santorini in 1520 BC

Tsunamis are most common in the Pacific Ocean, but some scientists believe that in 1520 BC, a volcanic explosion destroyed much of the island of Santorini (also known as Thera) in the eastern Mediterranean. This set off a *tsunami* that engulfed the coast of Crete, wiping out the Minoan civilization and thereby changing the course of history. This may well be one of the origins of the legend of the lost underwater continent of Atlantis.

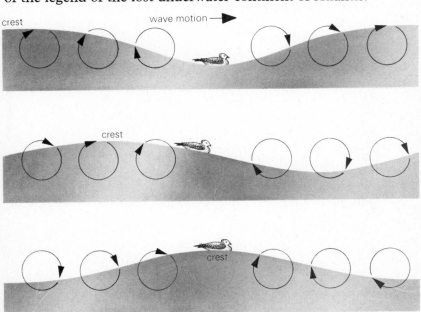

Ocean

Earth

Without the moon (right) there would be no tides. With the moon (below) the picture changes. The strong pull on the side of the earth facing the moon produces a bulge in the ocean water.

The medium pull in the middle tugs at the body of the earth itself pulling the earth towards the moon. This leaves behind another bulge of ocean water on the side of the earth opposite the moon. It is left behind because it is farthest away from the moon where the pulling forces are weakest.

Moon

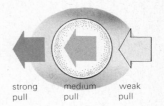

strong pull | medium pull | weak pull

The daily up-and-down movement of the tides is caused by the pull of the moon. Everything in space is pulling at everything else. We call this pulling force gravity. The earth's gravity keeps our feet on the ground and the moon in its orbit around us. In turn the moon is tugging at us. This pulling force is very small but the nearer we are to the moon, the greater it is. Thus on the side of the earth facing the moon the tug is greatest, while on the opposite side, which is further away, it is weaker. The diagram above has been greatly exaggerated to show the two bulges of water which the moon produces.

In the open ocean the volume of water contained in the bulges is spread widely and the difference between high and low tide is only about a metre (3 feet). When a bulge pours into a narrow sea like the English Channel it gets squeezed at the edges. Since it cannot go down, it goes up, and the difference between high and low tides in these narrow channels is much greater. In Fundy Bay, Nova Scotia, the sea level may change by as much as 16.4 metres (53.5 feet) between tides.

Moon

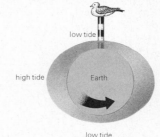

low tide

high tide | Earth

low tide

Moon

About 6 hours later

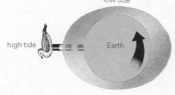

high tide | Earth

low tide

Drilling for oil and gas in the North Sea ▶

Energy and Minerals

At the mouth of the river Rance in France the twice daily movement of the tides is used to generate electricity. The water moving in and out of the estuary turns the turbines of the world's first tidal power station.

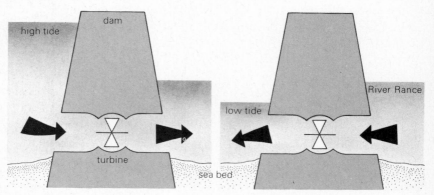

How the French tidal power station works: at high tide the water flows into the River Rance turning the blades of the turbines which make electricity. At low tide the process is reversed; the water level in the river is now higher than the level of the sea and the water flows out.

The daily tidal movements are the most recent energy source that man has learned to use. As long ago as 1620, miners in Scotland began to tunnel under the sea bed in search of coal. Iron, copper, nickel, and tin ore, are also extracted from beneath the sea through tunnels burrowed out from the coast. Modern tunnelling techniques make it possible to extend these shafts as far as 48 kilometres (30 miles) out to sea, but to reach the minerals far out in the sea bed we will have to think of some new way of extracting them.

The whole margin of the ocean basin, from the continental shelf down to the continental rise, is rich in energy-producing minerals such as coal, oil, and gas, and other important minerals are found in the sand-and-mud sediments on the sea bed. Today, in several parts of the world, including the North Sea, giant drilling platforms are being erected to extract vast quantities of oil and natural gas from the rock layers beneath the sea floor.

Each cubic kilometre (about one-quarter of a cubic mile) of sea water contains 41 million tonnes of dissolved salts. Much of this is common table salt, sodium chloride, but all the chemical elements are present. The earth's 1,352,000,000 cubic kilometres (330,000,000 cubic miles) of sea water form a vast store of mineral wealth.

Stone Age men began extracting this salt from the sea thousands of years ago by trapping sea water in shallow basins; the sun evaporated the water, leaving the salt behind. Today we still get our salt in much the same way, though we also extract the metal magnesium and the gas bromine from the salt: magnesium is a lightweight metal which has many uses, while bromine is added to petrol to improve engine performance. The table below shows the mineral content of one cubic kilometre of sea water.

Element	Tonnes per cubic kilometre (approx.)	Element	Tonnes per cubic kilometre (approx.)	Element	Tonnes per cubic kilometre (approx.)
Chlorine	22,375,000	Indium	24	Silver	0.25
Sodium	12,375,000	Zinc	12	Lanthanun	0.25
Magnesium	1,600,000	Iron	12	Krypton	0.25
Sulphur	1,050,000	Aluminium	12	Neon	0.125
Calcium	475,000	Molybdenum	12	Cadmium	0.125
Potassium	450,000	Selenium	5	Tungsten	0.125
Bromine	76,000	Tin	3.5	Xenon	0.125
Carbon	33,000	Copper	3.5	Germanium	0.075
Strontium	9,500	Arsenic	3.5	Chromium	0.05
Boron	5,750	Uranium	3.5	Thorium	0.05
Silicon	3,500	Nickel	2.25	Scandium	0.05
Fluorine	1,525	Vanadium	2.25	Lead	0.025
Argon	700	Manganese	2.25	Mercury	0.025
Nitrogen	600	Titanium	1.25	Gallium	0.025
Lithium	200	Antimony	0.5	Bismuth	0.025
Rubidium	143	Cobalt	0.5	Niobium	0.0125
Phosphorus	83	Caesium	0.5	Thalium	0.0125
Iodine	70	Cerium	0.5	Helium	0.0075
Barium	35	Yttrium	0.25	Gold	0.005

The gold alone is worth about £2,580 (about US$6,450), but to extract the 41 million tonnes of salts would mean building a factory capable of processing 2,600,000 litres (520,000 gallons) of sea water every minute for one year. That would be unbelievably expensive today, but perhaps in the future it might be worth while. For the present there are more than enough mineral-rich mud-and-sand sediments waiting to be discovered on the ocean floor.

Frogmen prospecting the sea floor ▶

Oceans: Facts and Figures

	Area		Greatest Depth	
	square kilometres	square miles	metres	feet
Pacific Ocean	163,469,000	63,855,000	11,070	36,198
Atlantic Ocean	81,265,000	31,744,000	8,409	27,498
Indian Ocean	72,630,000	28,371,000	8,073	26,400
Artic Ocean	13,893,000	5,427,000	5,468	17,880
Mediterranean Sea	2,475,000	967,000	4,862	15,900
South China Sea	2,291,000	895,000	5,532	18,090
Bering Sea	2,243,000	876,000	5,138	16,800
Caribbean Sea	1,920,000	750,000	7,517	24,580
Gulf of Mexico	1,526,000	596,000	4,391	14,360
Sea of Okhotsk	1,510,000	590,000	3,487	11,400
East China Sea	1,233,000	482,000	3,009	9,840
Hudson Bay	1,219,000	476,000	260	850
Sea of Japan	996,000	389,000	3,755	12,280
North Sea	568,000	222,000	664	2,170
Black Sea	456,000	178,000	2,251	7,360
Red Sea	433,000	169,000	2,254	7,370
Baltic Sea	417,000	163,000	440	1,440

Total volume: 1,352,000,000 cubic kilometres (330,000,000 cubic miles).

Total weight: 1,300,000,000,000,000,000 tonnes.

44

For many centuries man has gazed out to sea from the decks of ships and the shores of his dry-land home. Today he can even look down from space at his blue planet and see the vastness of the unexplored territory that awaits him. From his first home in Africa man has spread throughout the world: he lives in deserts where there is little water, in frozen places where there is little warmth, and in high mountain areas where there is less oxygen than at sea level. Now he is learning to survive in space and under water, taking his air, food and warmth with him wherever he goes. The ocean world still holds many of its secrets, but the further exploration and settlement of its depths promises to be as challenging and rewarding as were those first great voyages of discovery across its surface. And maybe, within our lifetimes, some of us will be living in cities on the ocean floor.

A view of the Pacific Ocean from space.
Lower California can be seen to the left
of the white question-mark-shaped
cloud formation at the top of the picture.
You can also see the whole of South America.

An underwater city of the future ▶

Index